to disembark

Gwendolyn Brooks

THIRD WORLD PRESS, CHICAGO

to disembark

Third World Press
7524 South Cottage Grove Ave.
Chicago, IL 60619

Fourth Printing
Printed in the United States of America
Cover art & Design by Adjoa Jackson

Library of Congress Cataloguing in Publication data

Brooks, Gwendolyn

1. Title   Poetry

ISBN 0-88378-101-8 (cloth)
ISBN 0-88378-102-6 (paper)

Acknowledgments

To Broadside Press

    Original Publication of *Riot, Family Pictures and Beckonings*

To Ebony

    Original Publication of *Another Preachment to Blacks,* first published under the name *Boys Black*

To Dudley Randall.
With Affection and Respect.

IN MEMORIAM: EDGAR WILLIAM BLAKELY
January 10, 1919—December 25, 1980

A friend is one
to whom you can say too much.

That was the title and text of Edgar Blakely, our
rich-humored, raw and ready,
righteous and radiant running-buddy—
responsible to
community and heart.

The document of his living is
out and plain,
level and direct. "Be sane. Be
neighbor to all the people in the world."

Gwendolyn
Friday, December 26, 1980

CONTENTS

1

riot

RIOT

A Poem in Three Parts

> A riot is the language of the unheard.
> --Martin Luther King, Jr.

John Cabot, out of Wilma, once a Wycliffe,
all whitebluerose below his golden hair,
wrapped richly in right linen and right wool,
almost forgot his Jaguar and Lake Bluff;
almost forgot Grandtully (which is The
Best Thing That Ever Happened To Scotch); almost
forgot the sculpture at the Richard Gray
and Distelheim; the kidney pie at Maxim's,
the Grenadine de Beouf at Maison Henri.

Because the "Negroes" were coming down the street.

Because the Poor were sweaty and unpretty
(not like Two Dainty Negroes in Winnetka)
and they were coming toward him in rough ranks.
In seas. In windsweep. They were black and loud.
And not detainable. And not discreet.

Gross. Gross. "Que tu es grossier!" John Cabot
itched instantly beneath the nourished white
that told his story of glory to the World.
"Don't let It touch me! the blackness! Lord!" he
whispered to any handy angel in the sky.

But, in a thrilling announcement, on It drove
and breathed on him: and touched him. In that breath
the fume of pig foot, chitterling and cheap chili,
malign, mocked John. And, in terrific touch, old
averted doubt jerked forward decently,
cried "Cabot! John! You are a desperate man,
and the desperate die expensively today."

John Cabot went down in the smoke and fire
and broken glass and blood, and he cried "Lord!
Forgive these nigguhs that know not what they do."

The Third Sermon on the Warpland

Phoenix:
"In Egyptian mythology,
a bird which lived for five hundred
years and then consumed itself in fire,
rising renewed from the ashes."
--Webster.

The earth is a beautiful place.
Watermirrors and things to be reflected.
Goldenrod across the little lagoon.

The Black Philosopher says
"Our chains are in the keep of the keeper
in a labeled cabinet
on the second shelf by the cookies,
sonatas, the arabesques ...
There's a rattle, sometimes.
You do not hear it who mind only
cookies and crunch them.

You do not hear the remarkable music -- 'A
Death Song For You Before You Die.'
If you could hear it
you would make music too.
The **black**blues."

West Madison Street.
In "Jessie's Kitchen"
nobody's eating Jessie's Perfect Food.
Crazy flowers
cry up across the sky, spreading
and hissing **This is**

it.

The young men run.
They will not steal Bing Crosby but will steal
Melvin Van Peebles who made Lillie
a thing of Zampoughi a thing of red wiggles and trebles
(and I know there are twenty wire stalks sticking out
of her head
as her underfed haunches jerk jazz.)

A clean riot is not one in which little rioters
long-stomped, long-straddled, BEANLESS
but knowing no Why
go steal in hell
a radio, sit to hear James Brown
and Mingus, Young-Holt, Coleman, John,
        on V.O.N.
and sun themselves in Sin.

However, what
is going on
is going on.

Fire.
That is their way of lighting candles in the darkness.
A White Philosopher said
"It is better to light one candle than curse the darkness."
        These candles curse--
inverting the deeps of the darkness.

GUARD HERE, GUNS LOADED .
The young men run.
The children in ritual chatter
scatter upon
their Own and old geography.

The Law comes sirening across the town.

A woman is dead.
Motherwoman.
She lies among the boxes
(that held the haughty hats, the Polish sausages)
in newish, thorough, firm virginity
as rich as fudge is if you've had five pieces.
Not again shall she
partake of steak
on Christmas mornings, nor of nighttime
chicken and wine at Val Gray Ward's
nor say
of Mr. Beetley, Exit Jones, Junk Smith
nor neat New-baby Williams (man-to-many)
"He treat me right."

That was a gut gal.

"We'll do an us!" yells Yancey, a twittering twelve.
"Instead of your deathintheafternoon,
kill 'em, bull!
kill 'em, bull!"

The Black Philosopher blares
"I tell you, **exhaustive** black integrity
would assure a blackless America...."

Nine die, Sun-Times will tell
and will tell too
in small black-bordered oblongs **"Rumor? check it
at** 744-4111.**"**

A Poem to Peanut.
"Coooooool!" purrs Peanut. Peanut is
Richard—a Ranger and a gentleman.
A Signature. A Herald. And a Span.
This Peanut will not let his men explode.
And Rico will not.
Neither will Sengali.
Nor Bop nor Jeff, Geronimo nor Lover.
These merely peer and purr,
and pass the Passion over.
The Disciples stir
and thousandfold confer
with ranging Rangermen;
mutual in their "Yeah!—
this AIN'T all upinheah!"

"But WHY do These People offend **themselves?**" say they
who say also "It's time.
It's time to help
These People."

Lies are told and legends made.
Phoenix rises unafraid.

The Black Philosopher will remember:
"There they came to life and exulted,
the hurt mute.
Then it was over.

The dust, as they say, settled."

AN ASPECT OF LOVE, ALIVE IN THE ICE AND FIRE

LaBohem Brown

In a package of minutes there is this We.
How beautiful.
Merry foreigners in our morning,
we laugh, we touch each other,
are responsible props and posts.

A physical light is in the room.

Because the world is at the window
we cannot wonder very long.

You rise. Although
genial, you are in yourself again.
I observe
your direct and respectable stride.
You are direct and self-accepting as a lion
in Afrikan velvet. You are level, lean,
remote.

There is a moment in Camaraderie
when interruption is not to be understood.
I cannot bear an interruption.
This is the shining joy;
the time of not-to-end.

On the street we smile.
We go
in different directions
down the imperturbable street.

2

family pictures

THE LIFE OF LINCOLN WEST

 Ugliest little boy
that everyone ever saw.
That is what everyone said.

Even to his mother it was apparent—
when the blue-aproned nurse came into the
northeast end of the maternity ward
bearing his squeals and plump bottom
looped up in a scant receiving blanket,
bending, to pass the bundle carefully
into the waiting mother-hands—that this
was no cute little ugliness, no sly baby waywardness
that was going to inch away
as would baby fat, baby curl, and
baby spot-rash. The pendulous lip, the
branching ears, the eyes so wide and wild,
the vague unvibrant brown of the skin,
and, most disturbing, the great head.
These components of That Look bespoke
the sure fibre. The deep grain.

His father could not bear the sight of him.
His mother high-piled her pretty dyed hair and
put him among her hairpins and sweethearts,
dance slippers, torn paper roses.
He was not less than these,
he was not more.

As the little Lincoln grew,
uglily upward and out, he began
to understand that something was
wrong. His little ways of trying
to please his father, the bringing
of matches, the jumping aside at
warning sound of oh-so-large and
rushing stride, the smile that gave
and gave and gave—Unsuccessful!

Even Christmases and Easters were spoiled.
He would be sitting at the
family feasting table, really
delighting in the displays of mashed potatoes
and the rich golden
fat-crust of the ham or the festive
fowl, when he would look up and find
somebody feeling indignant about him.

What a pity what a pity. No love
for one so loving. The little Lincoln
loved Everybody. Ants. The changing
caterpillar. His much-missing mother.
His kindergarten teacher.

His kindergarten teacher—whose
concern for him was composed of one
part sympathy and two parts repulsion.
The others ran up with their little drawings.
He ran up with his.
She
tried to be as pleasant with him as
with others, but it was difficult.
For she was all pretty! all daintiness,
all tiny vanilla, with blue eyes and fluffy
sun-hair. One afternoon she
saw him in the hall looking bleak against
the wall. It was strange because the
bell had long since rung and no other
child was in sight. Pity flooded her.
She buttoned her gloves and suggested
cheerfully that she walk him home. She
started out bravely, holding him by the
hand. But she had not walked far before
she regretted it. The little monkey.
Must everyone look? And clutching her
hand like that....Literally pinching
it....

At seven, the little Lincoln loved
the brother and sister who
moved next door. Handsome. Well-
dressed. Charitable, often, to him. They
enjoyed him because he was
resourceful, made up
games, told stories. But when
their More Acceptable friends came they turned
their handsome backs on him. He
hated himself for his feeling
of well-being when with them despite—
Everything.

He spent much time looking at himself
in mirrors. What could be done?
But there was no
shrinking his head. There was no
binding his ears.

"Don't touch me!" cried the little
fairy-like being in the playground.

Her name was Nerissa. The many
children were playing tag, but when
he caught her, she recoiled, jerked free
and ran. It was like all the
rainbow that ever was, going off
forever, all, all the sparklings in
the sunset west.

One day, while he was yet seven,
a thing happened. In the down-town movies
with his mother a white
man in the seat beside him whispered
loudly to a companion, and pointed at
the little Linc.
"THERE! That's the kind I've been wanting
to show you! One of the best
examples of the specie. Not like
those diluted Negroes you see so much of on
the streets these days, but the
real thing.

Black, ugly, and odd. You
can see the savagery. The blunt
blankness. That is the real
thing."

His mother—her hair had never looked so
red around the dark brown
velvet of her face—jumped up,
shrieked "Go to—" She did not finish.
She yanked to his feet the little
Lincoln, who was sitting there
staring in fascination at his assessor. At the author of his
new idea.

All the way home he was happy. Of course,
he had not liked the word
"ugly."
But, after all, should he not
be used to that by now? What had
struck him, among words and meanings
he could little understand, was the phrase
"the real thing."
He didn't know quite why,
but he liked that.
He liked that very much.

When he was hurt, too much
stared at—
too much
left alone—he
thought about that. He told himself
"After all, I'm
the real thing."

It comforted him.

TO KEORAPETSE KGOSITSILE (WILLIE)

He is very busy with his looking.
To look, he knows, is to involve
subject and suppliant.
He looks at life—
moves life into his hands—
saying
Art is life worked with: is life
wheedled, or whelmed:
assessed:
clandestine, but evoked.

Look! Look to this page!
A horror here
walks toward you in working clothes.
Willie sees
hellishness among the half-men.
He sees
lenient dignity. He
sees pretty flowers under blood.

He teaches dolls and dynamite.
Because he knows
there is a scientific thinning of our ranks.
Not merely Medgar Malcolm Martin and Black Panthers,
but Susie. Cecil Williams. Azzie Jane.
He teaches
strategy and the straight aim;
Black volume;
might of mind, Black flare—
volcanoing merit, Black
herohood.

Black total.
        He is no kitten Traveler
and no poor Knower of himself.

        Blackness
is a going to essences and to unifyings.
"MY NAME IS AFRIKA!"
        Well, every fella's a Foreign Country.

This Foreign Country speaks to You.

TO DON AT SALAAM

I like to see you lean back in your chair
so far you have to fall but do not—
your arms back, your fine hands
in your print pockets.

Beautiful. Impudent.
Ready for life.
A tied storm.

I like to see you wearing your boy smile
whose tribute is for two of us or three.

Sometimes in life
things seem to be moving
and they are not
and they are not
there.
You are there.

Your voice is the listened-for music.
Your act is the consolidation.

I like to see you living in the world.

WALTER BRADFORD

Just As You Think You're "Better Now"
Something Comes To The Door.
It's a Wilderness, Walter.
It's a Whirlpool or Whipper.

THEN you have to revise the messages;
and, pushing through roars
  of the Last Trombones of seduction,
the deft orchestration,
settle the sick ears to hear and to heed and to hold;
the sick ears a-plenty.

It's Walter-work, Walter.
     Not overmuch for
brick-fitter, brick-MAKER, and wave-
outwitter;
whip-stopper.
Not overmuch for a
Tree-planting Man.

Stay.

YOUNG AFRIKANS

of the **furious**

Who take Today and jerk it out of joint
have made new underpinnings and a Head.

Blacktime is time for chimeful
 poemhood
but they decree a
Jagged chiming now.

If there are flowers flowers
must come out to the road. Rowdy! —
knowing where wheels and people are,
knowing where whips and screams are,
knowing where deaths are, where the kind kills are.

As for that other kind of kindness,
if there is milk it must be mindful.
The milkofhumankindness must be mindful
as wily wines.
Must be fine fury.
Must be mega, must be main.

Taking Today (to jerk it out of joint)
the hardheroic maim the
leechlike-as-usual who use,
adhere to, carp, and harm.

And they await,
across the Changes and the spiraling dead,
our Black revival, our Black vinegar,
our hands, and our hot blood.

PAUL ROBESON

That time
we all heard it,
cool and clear,
cutting across the hot grit of the day.
The major Voice.
The adult Voice
forgoing Rolling River,
forgoing tearful tale of bale and barge
and other symptoms of an old despond.
Warning, in music-words
devout and large,
that we are each other's
harvest:
we are each other's
business:
we are each other's
magnitude and bond.

SONG: THE REV. MUBUGWU DICKINSON RUMINATES
BEHIND THE SERMON

If possible,
sleep through the morning three-thirties of the world.
Agitation is general all over America.
Agitation is general all over all the known countries.
Agitation, presently, will be general through that Moon
to which in magic
those humans rose to register their science and their soil.
I wish I had a goodly word for you.
You want brief brandy, or a braver beer.
"Be good" is the good I know.
But that will not suffice because it
is neither heat nor ice; because it
is what you learned when, little and "a fool,"
you sat in Sunday School.

SPEECH TO THE YOUNG
SPEECH TO THE PROGRESS-TOWARD
(Among them Nora and Henry III)

Say to them,
say to the down-keepers,
the sun-slappers,
the self-soilers,
the harmony-hushers,
"Even if you are not ready for day
it cannot always be night."
You will be right.
For that is the hard home-run.

Live not for battles won.
Live not for the-end-of-the-song.
Live in the along.

3

to the diaspora

TO THE DIASPORA

TO THE DIASPORA
you did not know you were Afrika

When you set out for Afrika
you did not know you were going.
Because
you did not know you were Afrika.
You did not know the Black continent
that had to be reached
was you.

I could not have told you then that some sun
would come,
somewhere over the road,
would come evoking the diamonds
of you, the Black continent—
somewhere over the road.
You would not have believed my mouth.

When I told you, meeting you somewhere close
to the heat and youth of the road,
liking my loyalty, liking belief,
you smiled and you thanked me but very little believed me.

Here is some sun. Some.
Now off into the places rough to reach.
Though dry, though drowsy, all unwillingly a-wobble,
into the dissonant and dangerous crescendo.
Your work, that was done, to be done to be done to be done.

MUSIC FOR MARTYRS

> Steve Biko, killed in South Afrika
> for loving his people.

I feel a regret, Steve Biko.
I am sorry, Steve Biko.
    Biko the Emerger
laid low.

Now for the shapely American memorials.
The polished tears.
The timed tempest.
The one-penny poems.
The hollow guitars.
The joke oh jaunty.
The vigorous veal-stuffed voices.
The singings, the white lean lasses with streaming
  yellow hair.
Now for the organized nothings.
Now for the weep-words.

Now for the rigid recountings
of your tracts, your triumphs, your tribulations.

A WELCOME SONG FOR LAINI NZINGA

Born November 24, 1975

Hello, little Sister.
Coming through the rim of the world.
We are here! to meet you and to mold and to maintain you.
With excited eyes we see you.
With welcoming ears we hear the
clean sound of new language.
The language of Laini Nzinga.
We love and we receive you as our own.

TO BLACK WOMEN

Sisters,
where there is cold silence—
no hallelujahs, no hurrahs at all, no handshakes,
no neon red or blue, no smiling faces—
prevail.
Prevail across the editors of the world!
who are obsessed, self-honeying and self-crowned
in the seduced arena.

       It has been a
hard trudge, with fainting, bandaging and death.
There have been startling confrontations.
There have been tramplings. Tramplings
of monarchs and of other men.

But there remain large countries in your eyes.
Shrewd sun.
The civil balance.
The listening secrets.

And you create and train your flowers still.

TO PRISONERS

I call for you cultivation of strength in the dark.
Dark gardening
in the vertigo cold.
In the hot paralysis.
Under the wolves and coyotes of particular silences.
Where it is dry.
Where it is dry.
I call for you
cultivation of victory Over
long blows that you want to give and blows you are going to get.

Over
what wants to crumble you down, to sicken
you. I call for you
cultivation of strength to heal and enhance
in the non-cheering dark,
in the many many mornings-after;
in the chalk and choke.

4

beckonings

THE BOY DIED IN MY ALLEY

Without my having known.
Policeman said, next morning,
"Apparently died Alone."
"You heard a shot?" Policeman said.
Shots I hear and Shots I hear.
I never see the dead.

The Shot that killed him yes I heard
as I heard the Thousand shots before;
careening tinnily down the nights
across my years and arteries.

Policeman pounded on my door.
"Who is it?" "POLICE!" Policeman yelled.
"A Boy was dying in your alley.
A Boy is dead, and in your alley.
And have you known this Boy before?"

I have known this Boy before.
I have known this Boy before, who
ornaments my alley.
I never saw his face at all.
I never saw his futurefall.
But I have known this Boy.

I have always heard him deal with death.
I have always heard the shout, the volley.
I have closed my heart-ears late and early.
And I have killed him ever.

I joined the Wild and killed him
with knowledgeable unknowing.
I saw where he was going.
I saw him Crossed. And seeing,
I did not take him down.

He cried not only "Father!"
but "Mother!
Sister!
Brother."
The cry climbed up the alley.
It went up to the wind.
It hung upon the heaven
for a long
stretch-strain of Moment.

The red floor of my alley
is a special speech to me.

TO JOHN KILLENS

THIS IS THE TIME OF THE CRIT, THE CREEPLE, AND THE MAKEITEER.

Our warfare is through the trite traitors, through
the ice-committees, through
the mirages, through
the suburban petals, through
toss-up, and tin-foil.

John Killens,
look at our mercy, the massiveness that it is not.
Look at our "unity," look at our
"Black solidarity."
Dim, dull, and dainty.
Ragged. And we
grow colder; we
grow colder.
See our
tatter-time.

You were a mender.
You were a sealer of tremblings and long trepidations.
And always, with you, the word kindness was not
a jingling thing but an
eye-tenderizer, a
heart-honeyer.

Therefore we turn, John, to you.
interrupting self-raiding. We pause in our falling.
To ask another question of your daylight.

A BLACK WEDDING SONG

This love is a rich cry over
the deviltries and the death.
A weapon-song. Keep it strong.

Keep it strong.
Keep it logic and magic and lightning and muscle.

Strong hand in strong hand, stride to
the Assault that is promised you (knowing
no armor assaults a pudding or a mush.)

Here is your Wedding Day.
Here is your launch.

Come to your Wedding Song.

For you
I wish the kindness that romps or sorrows along.
Or kneels.
I wish you the daily forgiveness of each other.
For war comes in from the World
and puzzles a darling duet—
tangles tongues,
tears hearts, mashes minds;
there will be the need to forgive.

I wish you jewels of Black love.
Come to your Wedding Song.

SAMMY CHESTER LEAVES "GODSPELL" AND VISITS **UPWARD BOUND** ON A LAKE FOREST LAWN, BRINGING WEST AFRIKA

"WEST SIDE," screamed Sammy Chester.
"I was born at 16th and Homan."
      I was BORN born born.

Unhalt hands—
body leantall rocking—
fierce innocent Afrikan rhythm....

West side. West AFRIKA.
Bursting back
free of the fiberless fury—
free of the
plastic platitudes—
free of the
strange stress, ordained ordure and high hell.

Afrika laughing through clean teeth,
through open sun, through fruit-flavored music that
applauded out of the other.

Afrika denied
Lake Forest limplush on that sunny afternoon.

ANOTHER PREACHMENT TO BLACKS

Your singing,
your pulse, your ultimate booming in
the not-so-narrow temples of your Power —
call all that, that is your Poem, AFRIKA.
Although you know
so little of that long leaplanguid land,
our tiny union
is the dwarfmagnificent.
Is the busysimple thing.

In the precincts of a nightmare all contrary,
wild thick scenery subdue.

Because
the eyeless Leaders flutter, tilt, and fail
The followers falter, peculiar, eyeless too.
Force through the sludge. Force, whether
God is a Thorough and a There,
or a mad child,
playing
with a floorful of toys,
mashing
whatwhen he wills. Force, whether
God is spent pulse, capricious, or a yet-to-come.

Beware the imitation coronations.
beware
the courteous paper of kingly compliments.

Beware the
easy griefs, that fool and fuel nothing.
It is too easy to cry "AFRIKA!"
and shock thy street,
and purse thy mouth,
and go home to thy "Gunsmoke", to
thy "Gilligan's Island" and the NFL.

ALSO AVAILABLE FROM THIRD WORLD PRESS

Nonfiction

*The Destruction Of Black
Civilization: Great Issues
Of A Race From 4500 B.C.
To 200 A.D.*
by Dr. Chancellor Williams $16.95

*The Cultural Unity Of
Black Africa*
by Cheikh Anta Diop $14.95

Home Is A Dirty Street
by Useni Eugene Perkins $9.95

*From Plan To Planet
Life Studies: The Need
For Afrikan Minds And
Institutions*
by Haki R. Madhubuti $7.95

Enemies: The Clash Of Races
by Haki R. Madhubuti $12.95

*Kwanzaa: A Progressive And
Uplifting African-American
Holiday*
by Institute of Positive Education
Intro. by Haki R. Madhubuti $2.50

*Harvesting New Generations:
The Positive Development Of
Black Youth*
by Useni Eugene Perkins $12.95

*Explosion Of Chicago
Black Street Gangs*
by Useni Eugene Perkins $6.95

*The Psychopathic Racial
Personality And Other Essays*
by Dr. Bobby E. Wright $5.95

*Black Women, Feminism And Black
Liberation: Which Way?*
by Vivian V. Gordon $5.95

Black Rituals
by Sterling Plumpp $8.95

*The Redemption Of Africa
And Black Religion*
by St. Clair Drake $6.95

How I Wrote Jubilee
by Margaret Walker $1.50

A Lonely Place Against The Sky
by Dorothy Palmer Smith $7.95

Fiction

*Mostly Womenfolk And A Man
Or Two: A Collection*
by Mignon Holland Anderson $5.95

Sortilege (Black Mystery)
by Abdias do Nascimento $2.95

Poetry

To Disembark
by Gwendolyn Brooks $6.95

I've Been A Woman
by Sonia Sanchez $7.95

My One Good Nerve
by Ruby Dee $8.95

Geechies
by Gregory Millard $6.95

Earthquakes And Sunrise Missions
by Haki R. Madhubuti $8.95

Killing Memory: Seeking Ancestors
by Haki R. Madhubuti $8.00

Say That The River Turns:
The Impact Of Gwendolyn Brooks
(Anthology)
Ed.by Haki R. Madhubuti $8.95

Octavia And Other Poems
by Naomi Long Madgett $8.00

A Move Further South
by Ruth Garnett $7.95

Manish
by Alfred Woods $8.00

New Plays for the Black Theatre
(Anthology)
edited by Woodie King, Jr. $14.95

Children's Books

The Day They Stole
The Letter J
by Jabari Mahiri $3.95

The Tiger Who Wore
White Gloves
by Gwendolyn Brooks $5.00

A Sound Investment
by Sonia Sanchez $2.95

I Look At Me
by Mari Evans $2.50

Black Books Bulletin

A limited number of back issues
of this unique journal are available
at $3.00 each:

Vol. 1, Fall '71   Interview with
                    Hoyt W. Fuller

Vol. 1, No. 3   Interview with
                    Lerone Bennett, Jr.

Vol. 5, No. 3   Science & Struggle

Vol. 5, No. 4   Blacks & Jews

Vol. 7, No. 3   The South

Order from **Third World Press**
7524 S. Cottage Grove Ave.
Chicago, IL 60619

Shipping: Add $1.50 for first book
and .25 for each additional book.
Mastercard /Visa orders may be
placed by calling 1-800-527-8340